INDIA

One Nation, Many Traditions

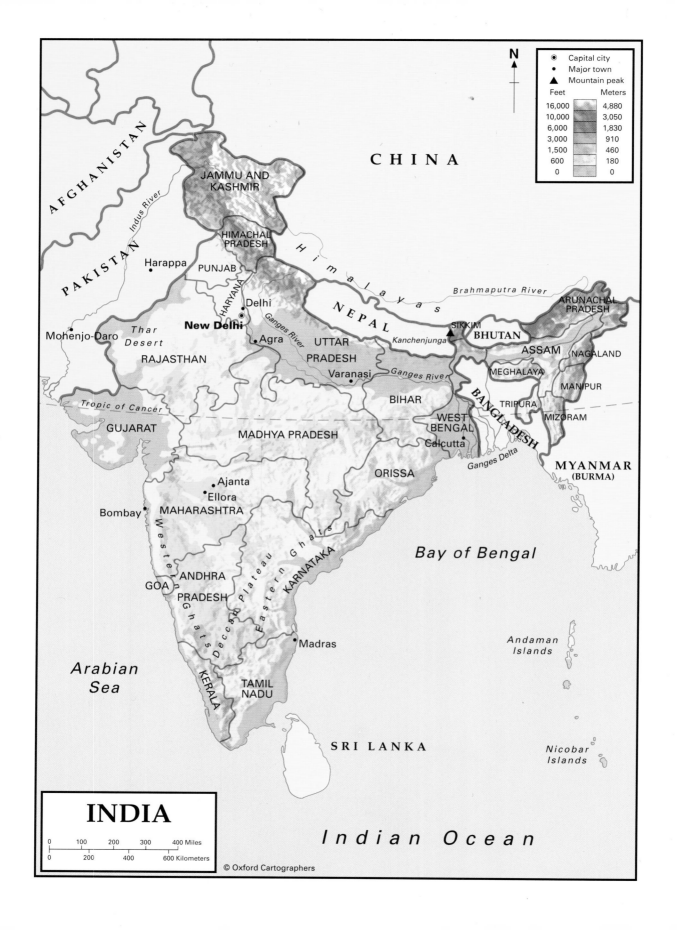

N

CHINA

AFGHANISTAN

JAMMU AND
KASHMIR

HIMACHAL
PRADESH

Indus River

PAKISTAN

Harappa

PUNJAB

HARYANA

Delhi

New Delhi

Mohenjo-Daro

Thar
Desert

Agra

RAJASTHAN

UTTAR
PRADESH

Ganges River

H i m a l a y a s

NEPAL

Brahmaputra River

Kanchenjunga

ARUNACHAL
PRADESH

SIKKIM

BHUTAN

ASSAM

NAGALAND

MEGHALAYA

MANIPUR

Ganges River

Varanasi

BIHAR

TRIPURA

BANGLADESH

MIZORAM

Tropic of Cancer

GUJARAT

MADHYA PRADESH

WEST
BENGAL

Calcutta

Ganges Delta

MYANMAR
(BURMA)

ORISSA

Ajanta

Ellora

MAHARASHTRA

Bombay

Deccan Plateau

Western Ghats

Eastern Ghats

Bay of Bengal

Andaman
Islands

GOA

ANDHRA
PRADESH

KARNATAKA

Madras

Arabian
Sea

KERALA

TAMIL
NADU

Nicobar
Islands

SRI LANKA

Indian Ocean

INDIA

0	100	200	300	400 Miles
0	200		400	600 Kilometers

EXPLORING CULTURES OF THE WORLD

INDIA

One Nation, Many Traditions

Megan Cifarelli

BENCHMARK BOOKS

MARSHALL CAVENDISH

NEW YORK

*With thanks to Rochelle Kessler of the Department of Asian Art
at The Metropolitan Museum of Art in New York City
for her thoughtful reading of the manuscript.*

FOR MY PARENTS

Thanks also to the many participants in the soc.culture.india newsgroup on the Internet who responded thoughtfully to queries and requests for information. The insights about, and memories of, growing up in India that they shared were tremendously helpful. Thanks are also due to Joyce Stanton, the editor of this volume at Marshall Cavendish, for her faith, patience, and good humor.

Benchmark Books
Marshall Cavendish Corporation
99 White Plains Road
Tarrytown, New York 10591-9001

Library of Congress Cataloging-in-Publication Data
Cifarelli, Megan, date.
    India : one nation, many traditions / by Megan Cifarelli.
        p.   cm. — (Exploring cultures of the world)
    Includes bibliographical references.
    Summary: Traces the history of this enormous Asian country and describes the ways of life of its people who have many different traditions, religions, and languages.
    ISBN 0-7614-0201-2 (library binding)
    1. India—Juvenile literature.   [1. India.]   I. Title.   II. Series.
DS407.C55   1996
954—dc20   95-44125

Printed and bound in the U.S.A.

Book design by Carol Matsuyama
Photo research by Sandy Jones

Photo Credits
Front cover: courtesy of Anthony Cassidy/Tony Stone Images; back cover: courtesy of Hilarie Kavanagh/Tony Stone Images; title page: courtesy of Tom Stack & Associates; page 6: Bridgeman/Art Resource, NY; page 9: Spencer Swanger/Tom Stack & Associates; page 10: Chris Noble/Tony Stone Images; page 12 (*top and bottom*): Manoj Shah/Tony Stone Images; page 13: Tim Bieber/Image Bank; page 15: Borromeo/Art Resource, NY; pages 17, 48: Giraudon/Art Resource, NY; page 18: Art Resource, NY; pages 20, 54: Carl Purcell/WORDS & PICTURES; pages 23, 29, 46, 47: Michele Burgess; pages 24, 31, 37: Joe Vesti/VESTI ASSOCIATES, Inc.; page 26: Hugh Sitton/Tony Stone Images; page 28: Wanda Warming/Image Bank; page 32: Wolfgang Kaehler; page 35: M. Mahidhar/Dinodia Picture Agency, Bombay; page 39: Nicholas DeVore/Tony Stone Images; page 40: Anthony Cassidy/Tony Stone Images; page 42: Dinodia/Unicorn Stock Photos; page 44: Jeff Greenberg/Unicorn Stock Photos; pages 51, 55: Hilarie Kavanagh/Tony Stone Images; page 52: Craig Lovell/VESTI ASSOCIATES, Inc.; page 53: Victoria & Albert Museum, London/Art Resource, NY; page 56: The Pierpont Morgan Library/Art Resource, NY

Contents

Rama and his army of monkeys storm the demon Ravana's palace.

1

GEOGRAPHY AND HISTORY

India's Past and Present

Magical, Magnificent Rama

Many years ago there was in India a wealthy king named Dasaratha (da-sha-RA-tha). In spite of his riches, Dasaratha was very sad, for he wanted a son. He prayed to the gods, and in a flash of lightning a magic potion appeared. The king gave this drink to his wives, and soon had not one, but four sons. One of them, Rama, was the favorite in all the land. Dasaratha did not know that his new son Rama was really the god Vishnu. Vishnu had come to earth as a human being to save the world from an evil demon named Ravana, who had ten heads and twenty arms.

On one of Rama's many adventures he met a beautiful princess named Sita (SEE-tah). Sita's father had promised her hand in marriage to any man who could shoot an arrow from his enchanted bow. This bow was so heavy that no man had been able to lift it. Rama lifted the bow as if it were a feather, and sent an arrow flying like the wind. Rama and Sita fell deeply in love and married. To Rama, Sita was the most precious thing in the world.

Sita and Rama lived very happily together in the palace of Rama's father. But one day a shadow fell on their joy. An evil wife of

7

Dasaratha tricked the old king into sending Rama away. The king banished the couple to the forest. Filled with sadness, Rama and Sita left the palace. As time passed they became used to their forest home.

One sunny day Sita was gazing out the window and saw a beautiful golden deer. She showed it to Rama and, spellbound, he followed the radiant creature. Each time he drew close, though, the deer bounded deeper into the forest. In the heart of the darkest part of the forest, Rama shot an arrow. As soon as the tip of the arrowhead touched its golden coat, the animal vanished. A demon had tricked Rama! He raced back to Sita as fast as he could, but it was too late. While Rama was gone, the evil demon Ravana had kidnapped the beautiful Sita.

How would he ever find Sita? Rama's heart ached. He searched in the north, he searched in the south, the east, and the west, and still he couldn't find her. Finally, with the help of the King of the Monkeys and his wise adviser Hanuman, Rama discovered the palace of Ravana. It was on an island called Lanka, and Sita was inside, guarded by dozens of ugly demons.

Rama brought a great army to Lanka and stormed Ravana's palace. For days and nights the thunder of horses' hooves and the clash of weapons could be heard for miles around. Hundreds of demons were killed by Rama's soldiers, but still they could not free the princess. In desperation Rama reached for the spear that the god Brahma had given him. He threw the spear with all his might. With the help of the gods it pierced the heart of the evil Ravana, killing him instantly. Like magic, the demon army disappeared, and Sita was free! Rama thanked the gods for saving his beloved wife. Together they returned to his father's land, and ruled for many years in peace and happiness.

The adventure of Prince Rama is taken from the *Ramayana,* a myth, or story of the gods, in the Hindu religion. The myth is so long that when it is presented as a play every October during the festival of Dusshera, it lasts ten nights. Modern India is just as fascinating as its enchanting legends. Throughout the history of this enormous land, people of many different traditions, religions, and languages have come together. Today India is a country of great contrasts and fascinating traditions.

Mountains to Monsoons

India is a large country in the southern part of Asia. It borders Pakistan in the northwest; China and Nepal in the north; and Bhutan, Bangladesh, and Myanmar (once called Burma) in the northeast. The southern part of India is a peninsula, or land surrounded by water on three sides. The Arabian Sea lies to the west, the Bay of Bengal to the east, and the Indian Ocean to the south.

In the tall Himalayas, the best way to travel is by foot or on the back of a yak or donkey.

India has three main regions: the mountainous north, the plains, and the peninsula. Each region has a different geography and climate. Part of the Himalayas are in northern India. These mountains have the highest peaks in the world. Even today, the easiest way to travel and transport goods in northern India is not by car or train, but on the backs of donkeys, yaks, and camels. Winters in the mountains are very cold, and the snow piles high. Summers are warm and dry. Much of the world's tea is grown in the eastern part of this region.

South of the foothills of the Himalayas, the land levels off to form the northern plains. The hot and dry Thar Desert lies in the northwestern part of the plains, but to the east the land is well watered. Here three major rivers flow: the Brahmaputra (BRAH-ma-POO-tra), the Indus, and the Ganges (GAN-geez).

Dry winds sweep the Thar Desert, pulling moisture from the land and sculpting the sand into dunes as tall as 500 feet (150 meters).

The waters of the Ganges are sacred to the Indian people.

Because of the abundance of water and rich soil, the northern plains region of India is the most densely populated area of the nation. Summer is unbearably hot, but winter is cool and dry. Here the rivers flood every spring because of water created when the snow on the northern mountains melts. A system of huge dams has been built to contain these floods. These dams generate hydroelectric power, and give water to farmers all year round.

The Ganges delta, the muddy fertile area where the Ganges River empties into the Bay of Bengal, floods during monsoon season. Monsoons are heavy rainstorms that blow in every year from the Indian Ocean.

Most of the southern, or peninsular, region of India, is taken up by a huge, raised, flat area called the Deccan Plateau. Highlands rise on the east and west coasts of the plateau. These are called the Eastern Ghats and the Western Ghats. (*Ghats* [ghaat] is an Indian word that means "stairs.") The climate in the southern part of India is warmer and wetter than the climate in the north. Some coastal areas have as much as 428 inches (1,087 centimeters)—almost 36 feet (10.9 meters)—of rain every year! The average rainfall on the west coast of the peninsula, however, is about 80 inches (203 centimeters) a year.

Animals and Wildlife in India

Animal life in India is as varied as the shape of the land. The mountains of the north are home to yaks and wild ibex. Tigers roam the foothills of the Himalayas and the swamps near the Ganges delta. Elephants also live in the foothills, where for centuries they have been captured and trained to work for local rulers and landowners. Monkeys, snakes, leopards,

In 1969 there were only two thousand tigers left alive in India, but the creation of reserves has increased their chance of survival.

Wild elephants range widely in search of food and can become a problem to humans if they move onto cultivated farmland.

wolves, wild hogs, and even lions are still found on the plains and in the tropical rain forests. Domesticated animals include water buffalo, cows, sheep, goats, and chickens.

Many of the animals that once lived in the plains, valleys, and jungles of India are now endangered. Some, like the lion and elephant, were victims of hunters. Others were killed by farmers protecting their animals and crops. The Indian government has set up special places called nature preserves. There the animals can live freely, safe from human beings.

Crowded Cities

India is home to an enormous number of people—more than 900 million. Although most people live in small farming villages, many are crowded into large cities. The nation's capital is New Delhi, in the northern plains. New Delhi is really a suburb of the older city of Delhi. Varanasi (sometimes called Benares) is one of the holiest cities for Hindus. Located in northern India on the Ganges River, this city attracts pilgrims, or religious travelers, from all over India. Calcutta is the largest city in eastern India, with almost five million citizens.

Bombay, on a small island off the southwest coast of India, is the largest city in India. The name Bombay comes from the Portuguese phrase *bom bahia*, meaning "good bay." People from all over India come to this jam-packed city hoping to make their fortunes.

Varanasi, India's oldest city, has more than fifteen hundred temples, palaces, and shrines.

Emperors, Warriors, and Traders

The Indus Valley Civilization

A remarkable civilization began around 2500 B.C. in the valley of the Indus River. Archaeologists discovered ruins of marvelous ancient cities at places now called Harappa and Mohenjo-Daro. Archaeologists are people who dig in the ground for objects left by people from the past. The buildings, streets, and tools found at these cities show that the Indus Valley Civilization was very advanced. The people even had a system of writing, although experts have not been able to translate it.

The Early History of India

Around 1750 B.C. the Indus Valley Civilization came to an end. No one knows why. The great cities were abandoned and people began to live in simple villages. A people from the northwest called the Aryans started to move into northern India. Many of the traditions that the Aryans brought are still part of Indian life.

After the arrival of the Aryans—and for most of its history—India was divided into many small kingdoms. They were often at war. Once in a while a few brilliant rulers were able to unite large regions. These kings founded powerful dynasties and ruled great empires. A dynasty is a series of rulers who belong to the same family. Some of these dynasties lasted for centuries.

The first great dynasty in India was the Maurya (MORE-ee-ya). It rose to power around 320 B.C. By 273 B.C., the Maurya dynasty controlled a vast amount of land. The empire stretched from central India to the area that is now Afghanistan in the northwest.

Another great dynasty arose almost five hundred years later. It was the Guptas (GUP-tuhs). The Guptas ruled from A.D. 320 to 550. They conquered much of northern India and had power over nearly the whole subcontinent. Under the Guptas,

This beautiful carving of the Hindu god Vishnu sleeping on a cobra was created during the reign of the Guptas, around A.D. 500.

15

great works of art, literature, and architecture were created. Important advances in mathematics and science were also made.

New Rulers

Around the year A.D. 1000 Muslim soldiers from Turkey and Afghanistan invaded northern India. By 1200 all of northern India was ruled by leaders called sultans who lived in Delhi. The year 1526 brought a new wave of Muslim invaders: the Moguls. The Moguls swept down from central Asia. Their leader, Babur, brought his army of 12,000 men and the latest weapons: guns. He easily defeated the old-fashioned Indian army of 100,000 men and 1,000 elephants. By 1530 the Moguls had conquered most of northern India, and they later controlled most of the south.

History tells us that the Moguls were fierce warriors and fearless leaders. There was much more to the Moguls, however, than blood and gore. Their society was very advanced and well organized. They were often tolerant of other religions. They were lovers of art, and built magnificent buildings.

At the same time that Mogul emperors were conquering the north, European traders were coming to India. The first European to arrive was the Portuguese explorer Vasco da Gama in 1498. By the 1600s Portuguese, Dutch, and British merchants controlled the trade in Indian spices, fine silks, and cotton cloth. Later, the tea trade became important, too.

Around 1700 the Mogul Empire began to fall apart. Soon India was again divided into small kingdoms. Some were ruled by Hindu kings called maharajas (MA-hah-RAH-jahs), and others were ruled by Muslim princes called nawabs (na-WAABS). The Mogul Empire was no more.

The Mogul rulers of India loved art. They were known for their fine miniature paintings, like this one. It was made to celebrate the crowning of an emperor.

Since the 1600s the British had been involved in India. British merchants made huge sums of money in the Indian trade. In 1857 the British conquered all of India and made it part of the British Empire. The Indians, however, did not enjoy being ruled by the English. They felt that they were discriminated against in their own land, and struggled for independence. The most famous leader of the Indian independence movement was a lawyer named Mohandas Gandhi. His followers called him Mahatma, which means "great soul."

Gandhi began a policy known as civil disobedience. Following his example, Indian protesters were never violent but refused to cooperate with British regulations. Finally, after the end of World War II, the British agreed to leave. In 1947

The weakening of the Mogul empire during the 1700s eventually allowed the British to take control of India.

India became an independent country, governed by Indians.

The history of India since it gained its independence has not been entirely peaceful. There were violent uprisings when Pakistan separated from the rest of India and formed an Islamic state. Today there are still conflicts among the country's many different groups of people. India's prime ministers have worked hard to help all the people live together peacefully.

Modernization has improved the quality of everyone's

INDIAN GOVERNMENT

India is a democratic republic. It has a strong central, or federal, government that shares some powers with the local state governments. India's chief of state is a president, elected by the legislature, or Parliament. The true head of government, however, is the prime minister. He or she is chosen from the political party that wins the most seats in Parliament. The Indian Parliament has two houses: the Council of States and the House of the People. Everyone over the age of twenty-one can vote in general elections for members of the House of the People. Members of the Council of States are elected by state legislatures; a small number are named by the president. India's judicial system consists of a Supreme Court that interprets the constitution, as well as local and state courts. India is a member of the Commonwealth of Nations, a group of countries that were once part of the British Empire.

lives. New agricultural methods allow farmers to produce more food. When food prices stay lower, fewer people go hungry. Electricity has been brought to most parts of India. New roads make the transportation of goods and people much easier. More and more Indian children go to school every year. Better education will help improve the lives of all Indians in the twenty-first century.

An ox, decorated with cowrie shells, and his master pause in the streets of Agra, once a capital of the Muslim Mogul empire but now populated mostly by Hindus.

2
THE PEOPLE

The Many Faces of India

The population of India is one of the most varied in the world. For thousands of years foreign invasions and migrations have added to the mixture of peoples. In India today many groups still practice their ancient traditions and speak their own languages. In fact Indians speak more than two hundred languages and sixteen hundred dialects, or variations of these languages. As many as fourteen languages are officially recognized by the government. The main language of India, spoken by almost a third of its people, is called Hindi (HIN-dee).

Ancient Beliefs in a Modern Land

Ancient beliefs are still very important in modern India. Traditionally, Indian society was divided into groups of people ranked according to their importance, which we call castes. Each caste had different duties and occupations. The highest caste was that of the Brahmans, or priests. Next came the Kshatriyas (kuh-SHA-tree-yas), or warriors and princes. Merchants and farmers were Vaishyas (VAI-sh-yahs), and the lowest caste was that of the Shudras, the laborers. Lower than the lowest caste were the Untouchables, whose work involved handling "unclean" objects, like garbage or sewage. Even though discrimination based on caste is now illegal in India, many Indians still live, work, and marry within caste groups.

The caste system is actually one of the teachings of the Hindu religion. More than three-quarters of the people of India are Hindus. This religion is based in part on a group of ancient religious writings called the Vedas. The Vedas tell of the search for an ideal way of life, known as dharma (DHAR-muh).

According to Hindu beliefs, one must try to be honest and courageous, to serve others, and to be nonviolent. Many Hindus do not eat meat because they don't want to hurt animals. Hindus also believe in reincarnation, the rebirth of the soul into another body after death. What happens to you after death is decided by your karma, or your actions. Hindus believe that if your karma is bad, you could be born again as an animal, like a dog or cat, or even as a fly! If your karma is good, you will eventually reach a state of blessedness called *moksha*, and will not have to be born again.

Many Gods and Goddesses

Hindus worship many gods and goddesses. The most important gods are Vishnu, Shiva, and Brahma. Important goddesses are Parvati and Lakshmi. Hindus believe that statues of gods are not simply representations, but in a way hold the power of the gods themselves. In Hindu temples priests take care of these statues. They wake the god up in the morning, and they bathe, feed, and dress him. Every Hindu home has a shrine to the gods, where flowers and incense are offered and chants are recited. These daily rituals are called

Holy men, who give up their possessions and strive to develop virtue and strength of character, are deeply respected throughout India.

pujas. Many Hindu ceremonies use fire and water, which are believed to be sacred.

The second-largest religion in India is Islam. The name *Islam* comes from the Arabic word *al-islam.* It means total submission to God, or Allah. The religion was founded in Arabia

THE SACRED GANGES: HOLY WATER, DIRTY WATER

Hindus believe that all water is sacred. They believe it cleans the spirit as well as the body. The holiest water of all is that of the Ganges River. Indians come from all over the country to bathe in and drink the water of the Ganges.

The city of Varanasi on the Ganges is an especially holy place, a gateway to heaven. It is thought that a person who dies there is purified. Religious Hindus, therefore, try to go to Varanasi to die, and to have their ashes scattered on the Ganges at this special city.

It is very sad that not everyone is so respectful of this great river. Millions of gallons of pollution pour into the Ganges every day. People bathing in the river are in contact with poisons such as cyanide, arsenic, lead, zinc, and mercury.

The Indian government is trying very hard to clean the Ganges's waters. Perhaps it is not too late to save one of India's most precious natural resources.

In Varanasi steps have been built along the riverbanks of the Ganges so that people can bathe in the sacred river.

by Muhammad (A.D. 570–632), who is believed to be God's prophet, or messenger. People who practice Islam are called Muslims.

Another important Indian religion is Sikhism (SEEK-ism). Its founder was named Guru Nanak (GOO-roo NAAN-ak) (A.D. 1469–1539). Most Sikhs live in the region of northwest India known as the Punjab. Sikhs have traditionally been known as fierce warriors.

Many Indians practice Jainism (JINE-nuh-zem). Jains are entirely nonviolent. They eat no meat, and some even cover their mouths with cloth to keep from accidentally swallowing bugs. India is also the homeland of Buddhism, although few Indians are Buddhists today. The Buddha, whose name means "the enlightened one," lived in the Himalayan foothills around 500 B.C. He founded a religion based upon meditation and a simple life. Christians and Jews have lived in small communities in India for centuries.

Life in India's Villages

Although many Indians live in cities, three-quarters of the people live in small villages. The kinds of houses they live in vary from region to region. In the southern region of Tamil Nadu, houses are made from the bamboo and palm leaves that grow all around. The village builder makes a mud platform for the house, to keep the floor above floodwaters. The walls are made of woven bamboo mats tied to bamboo poles. The roof is made of bamboo and palm leaves. These houses are cool because breezes can blow through them, and they keep everyone dry during the rainy season.

In the desert of northwest India, villagers live in *bhungas*, or round huts, and in square buildings called *chokis*. These

A villager and her companions harvest tea. It takes many hands, and long hours of work, to pick the tea for which India is famous.

houses are built with bricks made of mud, dung, and straw. The platforms that keep the houses above occasional floodwaters also keep snakes out. The thick walls keep these houses cool, even when the outside temperature reaches 110°F (43°C). In these desert villages everyone sleeps in string hammocks.

In most villages the way of life is traditional. People live in the same ways that they have for hundreds of years. Every village has a carpenter, a storekeeper, a potter, a weaver, and maybe a mechanic. However, most villagers are farmers. Depending on the region they live in, farmers grow rice, wheat, spices, tea, sugarcane, or cotton. They also raise an enormous number of cattle, although not for beef. Hindus are not allowed to eat beef. Cows produce milk, butter, and cheese, and when they die their hides go to good use.

MONSOON! THE GIVER AND TAKER OF LIVES

Every year in July, the rainy season in southern India begins. Monsoon weather has arrived! Monsoons are storms that roar in from the Indian Ocean. The storms themselves, with rain and high winds, can be terrifying and destructive. The floods they cause can ruin farms, homes, and even carry away livestock and people.

If these storms are so frightening, why do the Indian people actually smile when they see the huge, fleecy clouds that carry the monsoons? Monsoons bring welcome relief from the burning heat of the summer months. More important, India's farmers depend on the rains for their water supply for the entire year.

Farming is hard work for everyone in the family. Young children pick tea with their mothers. They help feed the water buffalo and camels that are used to pull carts and plows. Families labor in the fields all day long. More and more farmers are learning modern methods that help them produce food for their families and even have some left over to sell. The Indian government gives them water for their crops, better seeds, and loans that help them buy tractors.

In these traditional villages several generations of a family often live close together. Cousins grow up side by side, so there are always plenty of playmates. Farming, housework, cooking, and child care are shared by everyone. A family in which grandparents, uncles and aunts, cousins, and other relatives are closely involved with one another is called an extended family.

Life in the Big City

Overcrowding is a big problem in India's cities. People live very close together, without many conveniences. The cities,

People living in the "snow mountain state" of Himachal Pradesh, in the Himalaya Mountains, farm during the warm months, raise livestock, and practice forestry.

however, offer more types of jobs than the villages do. With the right education and training, a person can be a doctor, a lawyer, a teacher, a government worker, a storekeeper, an office worker, or almost anything you can imagine. Many young Indians from the villages flock to the cities because they do not wish to be farmers or are tired of village life.

While the cities offer more opportunities, there is a serious shortage of housing. Hundreds of thousands of people live in slums. The largest slum in all of Asia is in a part of Bombay

28

called Dharavi (da-RAH-vi). The people who live there have no running water or electricity. As many as ten people may share a small room, and a hundred may share a toilet. On laundry day mothers and daughters must carry their dirty clothes to filthy canals, for that is the only water available.

Even worse, many families spend their entire lives without ever having a home. They are born, grow up, and die on the dirty streets of India's teeming cities. Many of these homeless people have jobs, even two or three jobs, but cannot even afford to live in a slum.

Many farmers, like this young man in the state of Rajasthan, use traditional methods to work the land.

Of course, not all of the inhabitants of the cities are poor. There is great wealth in cities like Bombay, Calcutta, Madras, and Delhi. Rich families have luxurious homes in the suburbs, with air-conditioning, television, microwave ovens, and many servants.

Getting around in India

When we think of traveling in India, we conjure up romantic images of maharajas riding on elephants. Today, however, ordinary people use all sorts of vehicles to get from place to place. In the country, few people own cars. Instead they travel by foot or in carts pulled by oxen. In the cities cars and pedestrians share the crowded roads with buses, taxis, bicycles, and rickshaws, which are carts pulled by men on foot or bicycle. For longer distances, though, there is nothing like the Indian railroad, the fourth-largest system in the world. India also has an extensive system of highways, and airlines link major cities.

"Bollywood"

What country has the largest movie industry in the world? Would you have guessed that it is India? Indian movies are often musicals, full of adventure and romance. Their stars are the richest and most famous people in the country. The movie industry in Bombay has the nickname *Bollywood.* Everybody in India, rich and poor, country person and city dweller, loves the movies. Indians living all over the world feel a little closer to home when they see Indian movies.

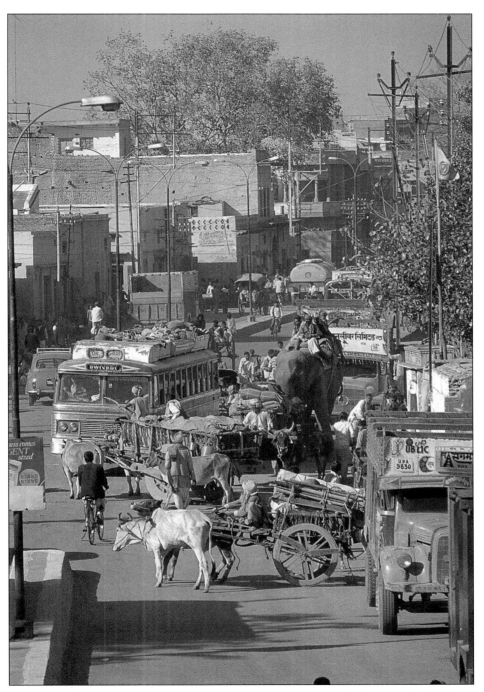

Bicycles, buses, pedestrians, ox-drawn carts—even an elephant—jostle for space in a traffic jam in Agra.

The life of an Indian child is marked by celebrations, rituals, and ceremonies.

3

FAMILY LIFE, FESTIVALS, AND FOOD

Indian Ways and Special Days

Although Indians speak many languages and have different customs, they all have one thing in common. Throughout the land the family is the center of everyone's life. Parents pay close attention to their children, and children try hard to make their parents proud of them. After eating dinner together, the family enjoys a favorite Indian pastime—chatting. They discuss their days at school and work, and parents tell their children stories about life when *they* were young.

A Woman's Place

Traditionally, Indian women have been wives and mothers. Marriages were arranged for young girls while they were toddlers and took place before they were teenagers. Men made all of the decisions. If their husbands died first, Hindu women were expected to commit suttee (sa-TEE). Suttee was a ceremony in which a widow committed suicide by being burned to death at her husband's funeral. She would lie down next to his body as it was about to be cremated, or set on fire.

In modern India women have more choices. Many choose

to be wives and mothers. In cities, especially, most jobs are still held by men. However, well-educated Indian women now have professional careers as doctors, lawyers, and professors. There has even been a female prime minister of India: Indira Gandhi.

Special Days

On special occasions—like the birth of a baby, weddings, and birthdays—families celebrate with friends and neighbors. In this large and varied country, there are many different customs for these special days.

In a Hindu Family

Twelve days after the birth of a new baby, Hindu families have a naming ceremony. They light twelve lamps around the baby's cradle, and the parents announce the new baby's name. On every birthday, the child is given presents, and the family asks the gods for his or her health and happiness in the year to come.

The next big day in the life of a Hindu child is set aside for boys. When a boy is between eight and twelve years old, he takes part in the Thread Ceremony. This ritual marks the change from boyhood to manhood. The boy and his father stand next to a sacred fire and the father places the sacred thread over the boy's right shoulder. The boy will wear the thread all his life. Family and friends come to watch this ceremony, and bring presents for the new man.

The most elaborate Hindu ceremony is the wedding. In traditional families the wedding is the first time the bride and groom will have met. During the wedding, which lasts for hours, the couple sit before a sacred fire, separated by a silk screen. After a priest reads from a holy book, he removes the screen, and the bride and groom finally see each other. The bride

A bride and groom at the end of a traditional Hindu wedding ceremony. Most marriages in India are arranged. Parents choose a person they feel will most closely match the background, social standing, and personality of their child.

then follows the groom around the fire seven times as the groom makes seven promises to her. After the ceremony the couple greet their guests and are host and hostess to a huge party.

At the end of life Hindus believe that cremation, or burning of the dead, frees the soul from the body. On the banks of a river the family builds a platform over a large pile of firewood. The body, covered with colored fabric and flowers, is placed on it. Then the fire is lit. Later, the ashes are scattered in the river.

In Muslim Families

As soon as a Muslim baby is born, someone whispers the name of God in its ear. Muslims believe that this should be the first word the baby hears. When the baby is seven days old, the family holds the *aqiqah* (a-KEE-kah), or baby-naming ceremony. At about the age of four, Muslim boys and girls have a ceremony called a *basmalah,* which marks the beginning of their education. Between the ages of seven and twelve, Muslim boys in India are circumcised. Muslims are married in a ceremony called *nikah.* There are prayers for many children, and a life of love. Unlike Hindus, Muslims bury their dead, with their heads facing toward their holy city of Mecca in Saudi Arabia.

Festivals and Holidays

Almost every day there is a festival somewhere in India. Every small village has its own feast day, while some holidays are celebrated everywhere. On all the holidays, families come together to celebrate ancient heroes, modern events, and the change of seasons.

India has two national holidays. August 15 is Independence Day, in honor of the day in 1947 when India became independent of Britain. Republic Day, on January 26, marks the anniversary of the beginning of the Indian Republic in 1950. Republic Day parades are held all over India. The most impressive one is in New Delhi. Old India meets new India in this colorful parade, as airplanes soar over the heads of graceful folk dancers and richly decorated elephants and camels.

Many festivals celebrated throughout India are part of the Hindu religion. The holiday of Dusshera, celebrated in the beginning of October, remembers the victory of Rama over the demon Ravana. This heroic Hindu story, part of which appeared in chapter one, is told in the poem *Ramayana*. All over India people put on costumes and act out this exciting myth.

Diwali is the Hindu New Year. This "festival of lights" comes at the end of October or the beginning of November, and lasts for five days. People place lamps called *dipas* (DEE-pahs) in windows and on rooftops. They believe the twinkling lights of the *dipas* will attract Lakshmi, the goddess of wealth, into their homes and businesses for the year. Diwali is a happy holiday season, a time to give and receive presents and to dress in new clothes.

Holi (HOW-lee) is another Hindu festival. Held in February or March, it celebrates the coming of spring. During this festival people run around in the streets splashing everybody

Everybody gets splashed with bright colors during the Hindu festival of Holi.

37

with colored water and powder. These bright colors are thought to scare away evil spirits. In southern India Hindus rejoice at the end of winter with a festival called Pongal. Children celebrate Pongal by flying kites.

Indians who are Sikhs also celebrate Diwali and Holi, but with different meanings. During Diwali, Sikhs remember a Sikh leader, Guru Hargobind, and his release from captivity. Following Holi, Sikhs celebrate spring with Hola Mohalla. On that day they act out legends from their warrior history.

An important Muslim holiday is Id-al-Fitr, "the festival that breaks the fast." It comes at the end of Ramadan, a month of prayer for Muslims. During this time they do not eat or drink anything between sunrise and sunset.

Food and Feasts

Every occasion in India is an excuse for a feast, and guests are always welcome. One thing that most Indian food has in common is that it is made with rich, aromatic spices, some delicate and some quite hot. The different climates in India are perfect

KELA AUR SANTRA KI LASSI (BANANA AND ORANGE SHAKE)

2 teaspoons sugar
1/2 teaspoon salt
2 small containers (10 ounces total) of plain yogurt

2 large bananas, peeled and sliced
2 large oranges, peeled and segmented

Mix the sugar, salt, and yogurt together.
Add the bananas and oranges, and stir until everything is well mixed. Serve, chilled, in a tall glass.

for growing a variety of spices, which are exported all over the world. The most common spices in Indian food are saffron, cumin, cinnamon, ginger, coriander, and chili peppers.

The staple, or most important, foods in India are wheat, rice, and lentils. The most common wheat bread is called chapati. A nutty-smelling rice called basmati is served with many different types of dishes. Lentils are cooked into a delicious stew called daal.

Northern India is famous for its tandoor cooking. A tandoor is an oven made from a giant clay pot. The pot is partially buried in the ground, and hot coals or wood burn in the bottom.

Vegetables for sale in a marketplace. Indian dishes contain lots of vegetables. Often they are the main ingredient, since many Indians do not eat meat.

Pieces of meat, usually chicken or lamb, are first soaked in yogurt and spices. Then they are placed on skewers, or sticks, and set over the fire in the tandoor. While the meat is being barbecued, the cook slaps bread dough on the inside of the tandoor. The bread cooked in a tandoor is called naan or roti.

Certain ingredients in Indian food are considered holy by Hindus. A butter called ghee is fed to statues of gods on their feast days, and cooked into sauces for holiday food. Ghee is very expensive. Only gods and maharajas can afford to eat it every day. Priests also feed milk and honey to the gods. Perhaps this explains the Indian love of sweets. Two favorite desserts are spiced rice pudding and *kulfi*, Indian ice cream.

Saris and Suits

The traditional cotton clothes worn by Indian villagers are practical in a country with hot weather. Village men sometimes wear dhotis (DOW-tees), which are loincloths made by wrapping a long, white cloth around the waist, then between the

Colorful saris—dresses made by wrapping the cloth about the body— delicate shawls, and lots of beautiful jewelry adorn these Indian women on a festival day

PAJAMAS: NOT JUST FOR SLEEPING

Did you know that pajamas were invented in India? *Pa jama* means "loose trousers" in Hindi. When the British were in India, they noticed many people wearing them. The British liked the loose trousers so much that they decided to wear them, too—but only when they were sleeping!

legs. Dhotis are cool and comfortable for long days of work in the fields. In the far south some men wear long, wraparound skirts called *lungis* (LUNE-ghees). Throughout India most women wear a wrapped dress called a sari (SAR-ee). Some northern Indian women wear Punjabi suits, with long trousers, a tunic, and a scarf. All over India, children often wear jeans, T-shirts, skirts, and blouses. When they are at school they usually wear uniforms.

In large towns and cities men wear Western-style clothing —suits for work and jeans for relaxation. Many women who work in big cities still wear saris, although some wear business clothes.

Religious traditions can affect clothing choices. Sikh men always wear turbans because their religion does not allow them to cut their hair. Muslim women wear dark, hooded cloaks called *burkas* to cover their heads and faces when they are in public. One of the most vivid reminders of the great contrasts in modern India is the sight of women in their *burkas* shopping in the gleaming, modern department stores of downtown Bombay.

About half of India's population can read and write.

4

SCHOOL AND RECREATION

Growing Up in India

In India parents and teachers expect children to work hard and to play hard. Most families value education, and put school and homework first. Children also have responsibilities around the house, like helping with dinner, setting the table, cleaning their rooms, even polishing their fathers' shoes. When all the work is done, Indian boys and girls are free to relax with the family or play with their friends.

Like children everywhere, Indian children look forward to seeing their friends in the classroom and in the school yard. The Indian government requires all children between the ages of six and fourteen to go to school. For the sons and daughters of wealthy families, there are fine, expensive private schools. India also has a system of universities and colleges that are excellent in science and technology.

In the large cities and towns, classes in public and private schools are held six days a week. Up to grade six, children study grammar and spelling, math, science, social studies, English, art, and physical education. Most students go to school through the tenth grade. Only those going on to college stay for eleventh and twelfth. At the end of high school those students who want to go to college must study hard and pass a difficult examination.

Almost every tiny village has a teacher, usually a villager who has returned after completing a university education. These village schools don't always have buildings in which to hold classes. When no building is available, all the children gather in front of the village store, or under a shady tree, to learn their lessons. In recent years, the government has set up a satellite-television system to transmit educational programs to these villages.

Unfortunately, many Indian children do not go to school every day. Although public school is free, some parents cannot afford uniforms, books, paper, and pencils. Also, many par-

Not all Indian girls get a formal education, but these students at a private girls' school in Bombay will probably have the opportunity to go on to a university.

ents rely on their children to help at home, on the farm, or in the family business. In all of India only about 70 percent of the children go to school. It is a sad fact that many parents think that it is more important for their sons to go to school than for their daughters.

Fun and Games

After school and work Indians like to relax and enjoy themselves. Children get together with their friends to play sports or cards, or to talk. In cities they can go to movies. Young men and women sometimes go out together in groups. However, there is little dating in India until about the age of twenty.

Walking through the streets of India's cities, one comes upon acrobats, wrestlers, snake charmers, jugglers, magicians, and puppeteers. All forms of modern entertainment are available to those who have money. Satellites send television programs from all over the world. Young Indians prefer cartoons, and their parents love to watch movies and game shows.

KABBADDI—A BREATHTAKING VILLAGE GAME

A team sport played by boys and girls in the villages is called *kabbaddi* (kah-bah-DI). *Kabbaddi* is a way of playing tag. A player from one team runs over to the other team's territory, and tags players on the other team. The player then tries to run back to his or her territory without being stopped by the tagged players. Does that sound easy? Well, there is a trick to playing *kabbaddi.* The player has to run there and back without taking a single breath! To prove that he or she hasn't taken another breath, the player has to shout *"kabbaddi-kabbaddi-kabbaddi-kabbaddi."* If the player makes it back, all the people who were tagged are out. When all the players on one team are out, the other team wins.

A snake charmer holds a python while two venomous cobras rise from their baskets. The snakes don't have ears to hear the music, but they feel vibrations and follow their handler's movements.

Many families go on vacation every year. Usually they will travel within India, sightseeing in ancient ruins, museums, national parks, and famous places.

For Indians of all ages, games of chance and skill, and playing and watching sports, are very popular. One of the most challenging games in the world began a long time ago in India—chess. Chess began in India more than a thousand years ago, in the sixth century. Chess was known then as *chaturanga*, and it was played by four players instead of two. Each player was in command of a group of game pieces, which looked like horsemen, archers, chariots, and elephants. Long ago, wealthy Indian princes played games of chess on huge fields, with their servants acting the parts of the chess pieces.

Which British and American sport was discovered in India? Polo. Polo was brought to India by the Moguls. The game, which is played on horseback, began as a training exercise for the army. It has been played by Indian princes and nobles for centuries, and it caught the eye of the British when they first came to India.

The British also brought their own sports to India. A favorite sport in India today, cricket, was made popular by the British. Cricket is a little bit like baseball, with a ball, bats, and runs scored. The game is played by local and neighborhood teams in every part of the country. It is also played professionally. During recess, Indian children often get together and play cricket, and many schools have their own teams.

An outdoor advertisement for one of India's favorite pastimes: the movies.

Field hockey, soccer (called football in India), badminton, and volleyball are also very popular. In these sports Indian teams play each other, and also compete internationally. India always sends teams to compete in the winter and summer Olympics. In recent years India has also had world-ranking tennis players.

It took great skill to create this beautiful, finely detailed miniature painting. It was made by an artist during the rule of the Moguls and was done very small, as a page in a manuscript, or book.

Ancient Arts
for a Modern World

Even in quiet villages modern ways are beginning to replace ancient traditions. Older Indians worry that the children of today spend more time watching cartoons than learning their local crafts and dances. Homes that once were filled with baskets and ceramics made by neighbors now have plastic and metal containers from faraway factories. Still, many Indians take great pride in their artistic heritage, and work hard to preserve their ancient skills.

Traditional Crafts

In Indian cities, towns, and villages, people create objects that are both useful and beautiful. Pottery is one of the oldest crafts. In every village, pottery is made with clay that is mixed in a pit by the potter's children, who stomp on the lumps until it is smooth. Pieces of wet clay are then placed on a quickly turning wheel. As the wheel turns, the potter's fingers shape and smooth the clay. When the pot is formed, it is often decorated with scratched or painted designs. It is then placed in a very hot oven called a kiln, where it is fired, or baked, overnight. Other

49

beautiful and traditional crafts are basket making, wood carving, and metalworking.

India has long been famous for its fine silk and cotton cloth. Lightweight, plaid cotton fabric is still called madras after the Indian city where it was first made. Other fabrics that began in India are muslin, calico, and chintz. Tie-dyeing, or making colorful patterns by tying fabric with string and dipping it in dyes, began in India, too.

Humble village homes in India are often elaborately decorated. In some regions brightly colored designs made of fabric are hung on the walls. In the deserts of Rajasthan (RAAJ-uh-stahn), the women and girls make patterns in mud plaster on the inside walls of their houses. The designs are whitewashed, and sometimes inlaid with colorful pieces of mirror and glass. The effect is very cool and beautiful.

Music and Dance

Music is considered to be the highest art in India. The Hindi word for music is *sangeet,* which means "putting it all together and expressing it." The human voice is considered the most beautiful instrument. Indian music is usually accompanied by a singer, who sings in a lilting, haunting tone.

The three parts of Indian music are called the raga, the tala, and the *suara* (soo-ah-ruh). The raga is the melody, which is played on a stringed instrument, such as the sitar. The tala is the rhythm or meter of the music, which is clapped or beaten on a pair of drums called tabla. The *suara,* sometimes called the drone, sets the pitch for the music. It is a constant tone played by a single instrument. Northern Indian music, called Hindustani music, and southern Indian music, called Carnatic music, use different instruments and have different sounds.

A musician, accompanied by a colorfully decorated elephant, takes time out to pose for the camera.

If music is the highest form of art in India, then dance is the most holy. The god Shiva (SHEE-vuh) is called the Lord of the Dance, because in Hindu mythology he taught the people how to dance. The most famous type of dance is called *bharata natyam.* The highly trained dancers have a sign language that allows their hands, feet, and bodies to tell the stories of Hindu mythology. The dancers, usually women, wear very elaborate

Their feet and hands painted red, these dancers tell a story with the movements of their bodies.

costumes and jewelry. Their hands and feet are painted bright red with a dye called henna.

In the Kerala region in southern India, the most popular dance is called Kathakali. A speaker recites a long story called the *Mahabharata* while the dancers act it out. All parts in Kathakali are played by men; women characters are played by young boys. The costumes and makeup are very elaborate and heavy. Kathakali dance is so difficult to perform that boys begin to train at the age of ten and must practice for ten years. In the past, Indian generals who wanted their troops to be strong and agile sent them to exercise with the Kathakali dancers.

Stories Old and New

Most of the traditional literature of India is religious or mythological. The oldest stories are the Vedas. The Vedas began as the songs or chants of priests, and much later they were written down in a language called Sanskrit. They tell stories of the Aryan gods and people. Hindu mythology is found in two great Sanskrit poems: the *Mahabharata* and the *Ramayana*. These are tales of adventure, magic, gods, romance, and right and wrong.

For most of India's history, books have been written in Sanskrit and various regional languages. Since the nineteenth century, however, many Indian authors have chosen to write in English. Mahatma Gandhi and India's first prime minister, Jawaharlal Nehru, wrote their autobiographies in English.

The story of Krishna and his love for Radha was a favorite subject for Hindu artists. In this painting, Radha stops a servant from cutting down the tree under which she met the divine prince. The prince sits in the room on the right.

53

Indian Arts and Architecture

Four thousand years ago, the ancient peoples of the Indus River valley were making beautiful sculptures. They also made tiny, carefully carved stones called seals. When pressed on wet clay, the seals made distinctive patterns. These patterns were used to mark people's property and goods for trade. The seals were also worn as jewelry.

The most magnificent sights in all of India are some Buddhist, Hindu, and Jain temples. These were cut like caves into the sides of cliffs, some more than a thousand years ago. The most famous of these man-made caves are at Ajanta and Ellora in western India. These remarkable caves are decorated with paintings and enormous sculptures. Religious Indians have always traveled long distances to worship in these temples. Today tourists come from all over the world to see them.

Some Hindu temples from about A.D. 1000 look quite different from these caves. They have tall, pointed towers called *shikharas,* and are covered with sculptures of plants, animals, and scenes from the lives of the gods. Working at the same time, the artists of southern India created beautiful bronze statues of Hindu gods. The most famous are statues of the god Shiva as Lord of the Dance.

This Hindu temple in the city of Madras is covered with incredibly detailed carvings.

54

THE TAJ MAHAL

One of the last Mogul rulers of India was named Shah Jahan. He had, as was the Mogul custom, many wives, and of all of them his favorite was named Mumtaz. She was mother to fourteen of his children, and was also his closest political adviser. Powerful and kind, she took care of the widows and orphans of the realm.

While Shah Jahan was away at war in 1631, Mumtaz died after she gave birth to her fourteenth child, a girl. Shah Jahan was heartbroken and built her a beautiful mausoleum, a building to hold her tomb. It took twenty thousand workers and one thousand elephants more than ten years to build it. Called the "Crown of the Palace," or Taj Mahal, after one of the royal titles of Mumtaz, this building in Agra is the most famous in all of India.

The Islamic rulers of India brought their own artistic traditions. They decorate their houses of worship, called mosques, with beautiful patterns and intricate designs. The Islamic architecture of India also includes tombs of the important rulers and religious men. The most famous Islamic building in

The Hindu warrior god Indra rides his elephant, Airavata, in this miniature painting.

all of India is the Taj Mahal (TAJH ma-hul).

Another form of art that was very popular in India during the Mogul rule is miniature painting. Miniature paintings are complicated and colorful, with many tiny figures. These beautiful paintings show scenes from popular tales, mythology, and court life.

Indian artists in the nineteenth century liked to imitate the styles popular in Europe at that time. In the twentieth century, however, some Indian artists have returned to their own traditions. Like its arts and crafts, India is a glorious blend of ancient traditions, customs brought by foreigners, and modern ways. The people of India, now the largest democratic nation on earth, celebrate the differences that make their land so rich and colorful.

Country Facts

Official Name: Hindi Bharat (Republic of India)

Capital: New Delhi

Location: in Asia; bordered to the north by Pakistan, Nepal, China, Bhutan, Bangladesh, and Myanmar. Arabian Sea lies to the west, Bay of Bengal to the east, and Indian Ocean to the south.

Area: 1,269,345 square miles (3,287,603 square kilometers).

Elevation: *Highest:* Kanchenjunga, Himalayas, 28,208 feet (8,598 meters). *Lowest:* sea level at coasts

Climate: tropical and subtropical for most of the country; rain forest in south and along eastern coast; semiarid desert in the state of Rajasthan; temperate in higher altitudes. Rainfall varies from almost none in Rajasthan, to 428 inches (1,087 centimeters) per year in Assam on the northeast coast.

Population: 911,600,000. *Distribution:* 26 percent urban; 74 percent rural

Form of Government: republic; member of Commonwealth of Nations

Important Products: *Agriculture:* rice, wheat, oilseeds, tea, coffee, cotton, jute. *Industries:* processed foods, textiles, steel, machinery, chemicals, jewelry. *Natural resources:* coal, petroleum, gems and minerals, iron ore

Basic Unit of Money: rupee; 1 rupee = 100 paise

Language: Hindi and English (official); Bengali, Gujarati, Kashmiri, Malayalam, Marathi, Oriya, Punjabi, Tamil, Telugu, Urdu, Kannada, Assamese, Sanskrit, Sindhi (all recognized by constitution); 1,652 dialects

Religion: Hindu (82.6 percent), Islam (11.3 percent), Christian (2.4 percent), Sikh (2 percent), Buddhist (0.71 percent), Jain (0.4 percent)

Flag: three horizontal bands: orange (top), white (middle), and green (bottom). A blue *chakra* (24-spoked wheel) is centered in the white band.

National Anthem: *Jana-gana-mana* ("Thou Art the Ruler of the Minds of All People")

Major Holidays: Dusshera (Hindu celebration of victory of Rama over demon Ravana, beginning of October); Diwali (Hindu New Year, end of October or beginning of November); Holi (Hindu festival marking coming of spring); Hola Mohalla (Sikh spring festival); Pongal (Hindu festival marking end of winter); Id-al-Fitr (Muslim holiday marking the end of Ramadan, date varies according to lunar calendar); Republic Day (January 26); Independence Day (August 15)

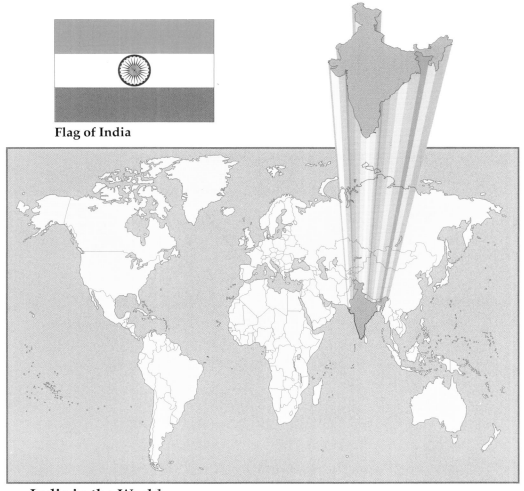

Flag of India

India in the World

Glossary

archaeologists (ar-KEE-ahl-uh-jists): people who learn about the past by digging up the remains of ancient cities and studying the tools, weapons, and pottery they find

civil disobedience: peaceful protest; refusing to obey laws that seem unfair by using nonviolent methods such as protest marches and strikes (refusing to work)

civilization: a form of society in which agriculture, trade, government, art, and science are highly developed. "Civilization" is often characterized by the use of writing and the growth of cities.

cremation: the burning, rather than burying, of the bodies of the dead

culture: the customs, beliefs, arts, and languages that make up a way of life for a group of people

delta: a region, usually shaped like a triangle, where a river empties into the sea. The river carries particles of soil and nutrients to the delta, making it muddy and often very fertile.

dynasty: a series of rulers who belong to the same family. A dynasty usually rules a nation over a long period of time.

empire: a group of countries, lands, or peoples under one government or ruler

Islamic (is-LAHM-ik): referring to the religion of Islam. People who follow Islam are Muslims, and they believe that there is one God, Allah, and that Muhammad is his prophet.

maharaja (MA-hah-RAH-jah): a Hindu king, or local ruler

Moguls (MOE-guhls): a people of central Asia who conquered India in 1526 and ruled there for centuries

monsoon: a very strong wind that blows in the Indian Ocean and southern Asia. In the summer, it blows from the ocean toward the land and brings very heavy rains. In the winter, it blows from the land toward the ocean.

Muslim: a follower of the religion of Islam (*see* **Islamic**)

nawab (na-WAAB): a Muslim prince, or local ruler

reincarnation (ree-in-kahr-NAY-shun): the belief in the rebirth of the soul into another body after death

ritual: a ceremony or act, often religious, in which several steps are followed very carefully

sacred: holy; belonging to God or a god

staple: a very important crop, like wheat or rice, that everyone in a region or country needs or uses

suttee (sa-TEE): the ancient Hindu custom in which a widow committed suicide by lying down next to the body of her husband as it was set on fire

turban: a head covering that is made by wrapping a long strip of cloth around the head several times

Western: referring to people and customs from Europe and North America

For Further Reading

Ali, Abdullah Yusaf. *Three Travelers to India: Being a Simple Account of India as Seen by Yuan Chwang (Hiuen Tsiang), Ibn Batuta, and Bernier.* Lahore: àl-Biruni, 1978.

Bains, Rae. *Gandhi: Peaceful Warrior.* New Jersey: Troll Books, 1990.

Braquet, A., and M. Noblet. *Tintin's Travel Diaries: India.* Tr. by Maureen Walker. New York: Barrons, 1992.

Ganeri, Anita. *Journey through India.* New Jersey: Troll Books, 1994.

Garnett, Emmeline. *Madame Prime Minister: The Story of Indira Gandhi.* New York: Farrar, Straus & Giroux, 1967.

Goalen, Paul. *India: From Mughal Empire to the British Raj.* New York: Cambridge University Press, 1992.

Kalman, Bobbie. *India, the Culture.* New York: Crabtree, 1990.

Masani, M. R. *We Indians.* Bombay, New York: Oxford University Press, 1989.

Meer, Fatima. *Apprenticeship of a Mahatma.* Phoenix, South Africa: Phoenix Settlement Trust, 1970.

Rice, Edward. *The Ganges: A Personal Encounter.* New York: Four Winds, 1974.

Singh, Anne. *Living in India.* Ossining, New York: Young Discovery Library, Editions Gallimard, 1988.

Wilkinson, Philip, and Michael Pollard. *Mysterious Places: The Magical East.* New York: Chelsea House, 1994.

Index

Page numbers for illustrations are in boldface

About the Author

Megan Cifarelli grew up in Columbus, Ohio. Ever since she was a child, she has been interested in the ancient arts and history of the East. Today she has a Ph.D. in Art History and Archaeology from Columbia University, and is a specialist in Mesopotamian art and archaeology. She works as a lecturer, a fellow, and a consultant with the Department of Ancient Near Eastern Art at The Metropolitan Museum of Art in New York City. Megan lives in New York City with her husband, Paul, and their two children, Charlie and Isabel. This is her first book for children.